Butterfly wings have it.

Triceratops had it.

The word **MOM** has it.

When you know

what to look for,

it's easy to start...

Seeing
SYMMETRY

written and illustrated by

LOREEN LEEDY

Holiday House • New York

Seeing
SYMMETRY

written and illustrated by

Loreen Leedy

Holiday House • New York

You might see
symmetry:

in the yard,

on a plate,

flying by,

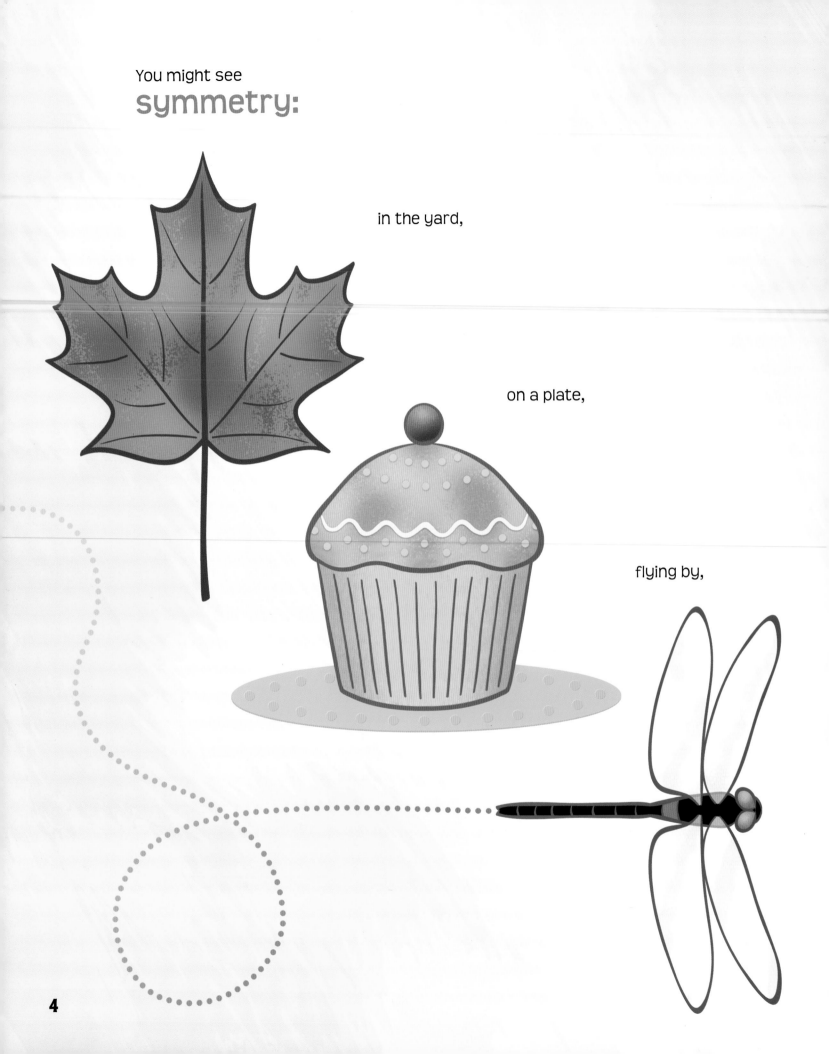

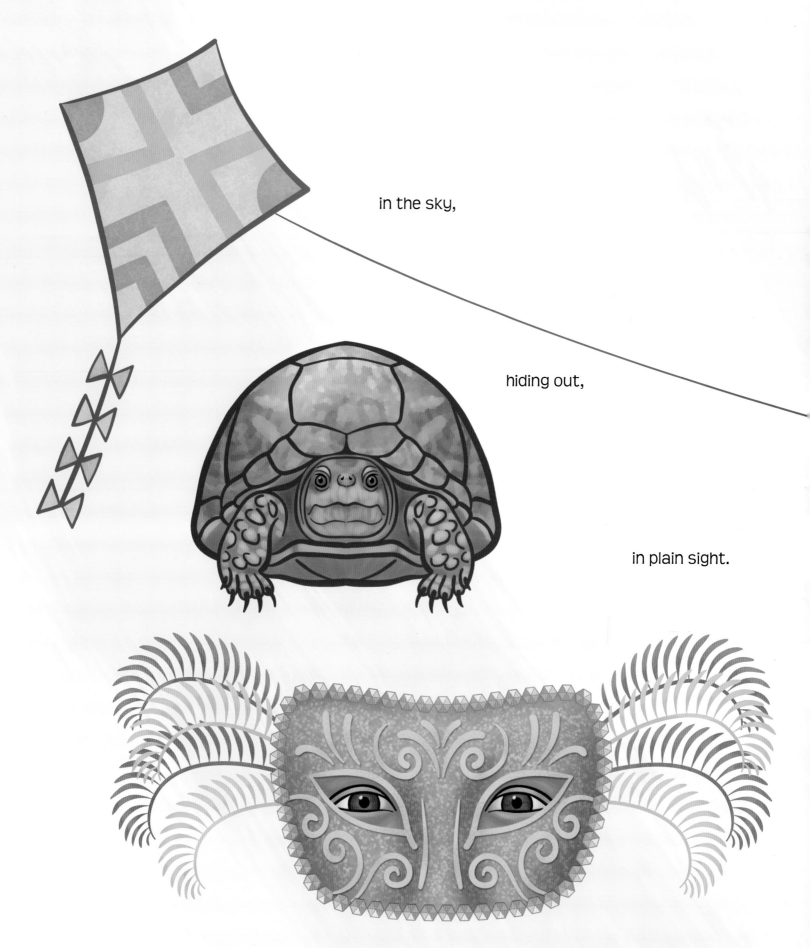

in the sky,

hiding out,

in plain sight.

So what is it?

If you can fold a shape exactly in half,

it has **symmetry.**

If each half is a
mirror image
of the other half,

the whole shape is
symmetrical.

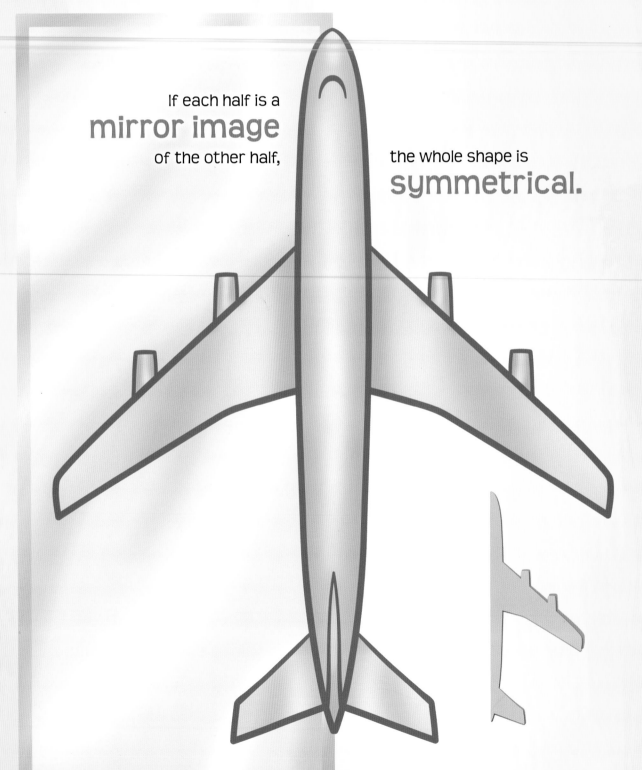

6

Each half is
flipped over
like a reflection.

The line in the middle is the **line of symmetry.**

Shapes such as these have **line symmetry.**

Are their other names for this kind of symmetry? See page 28.

If you could fold a sea turtle
from nose to tail,
the two sides would
match
flipper to flipper.

line of symmetry

It's impossible to fold a real sea turtle,
but one side of its body is the
mirror image of the other side.

*Nature is rarely exact—
one flipper may be slightly larger
than the other, for example.*

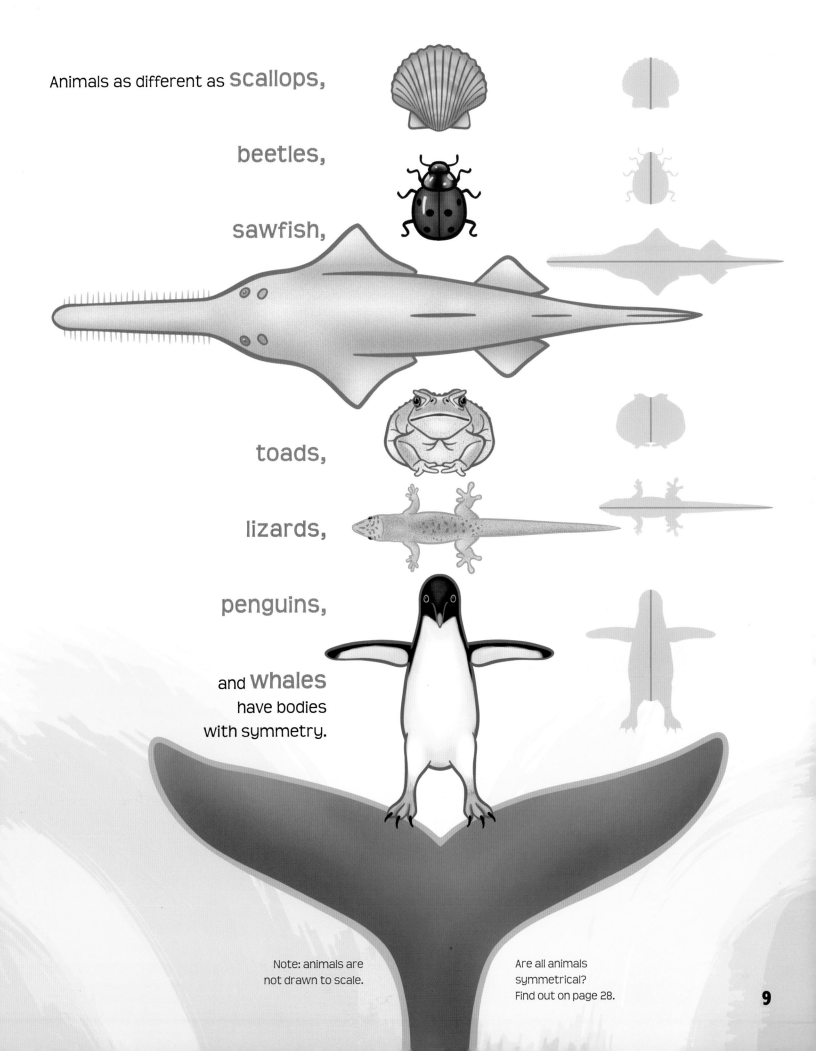

Animals as different as **scallops,**

beetles,

sawfish,

toads,

lizards,

penguins,

and **whales** have bodies with symmetry.

Note: animals are not drawn to scale.

Are all animals symmetrical? Find out on page 28.

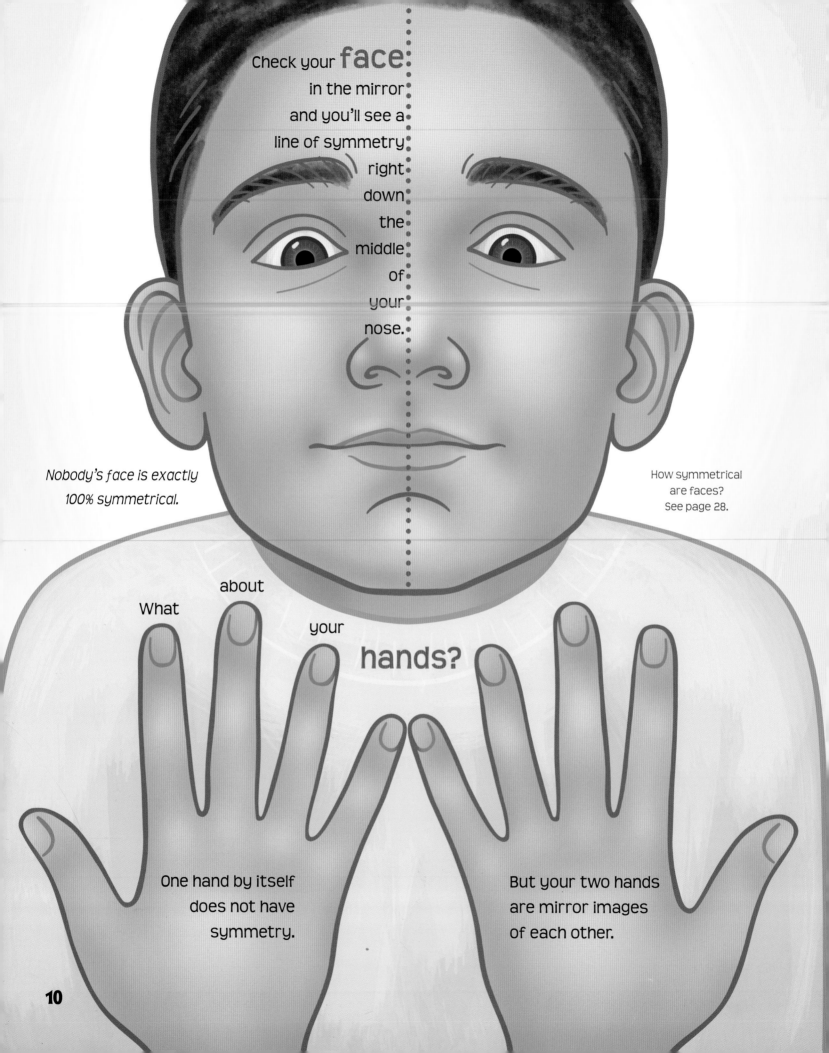

Check your **face** in the mirror and you'll see a line of symmetry right down the middle of your nose.

Nobody's face is exactly 100% symmetrical.

How symmetrical are faces? See page 28.

What about your **hands?**

One hand by itself does not have symmetry.

But your two hands are mirror images of each other.

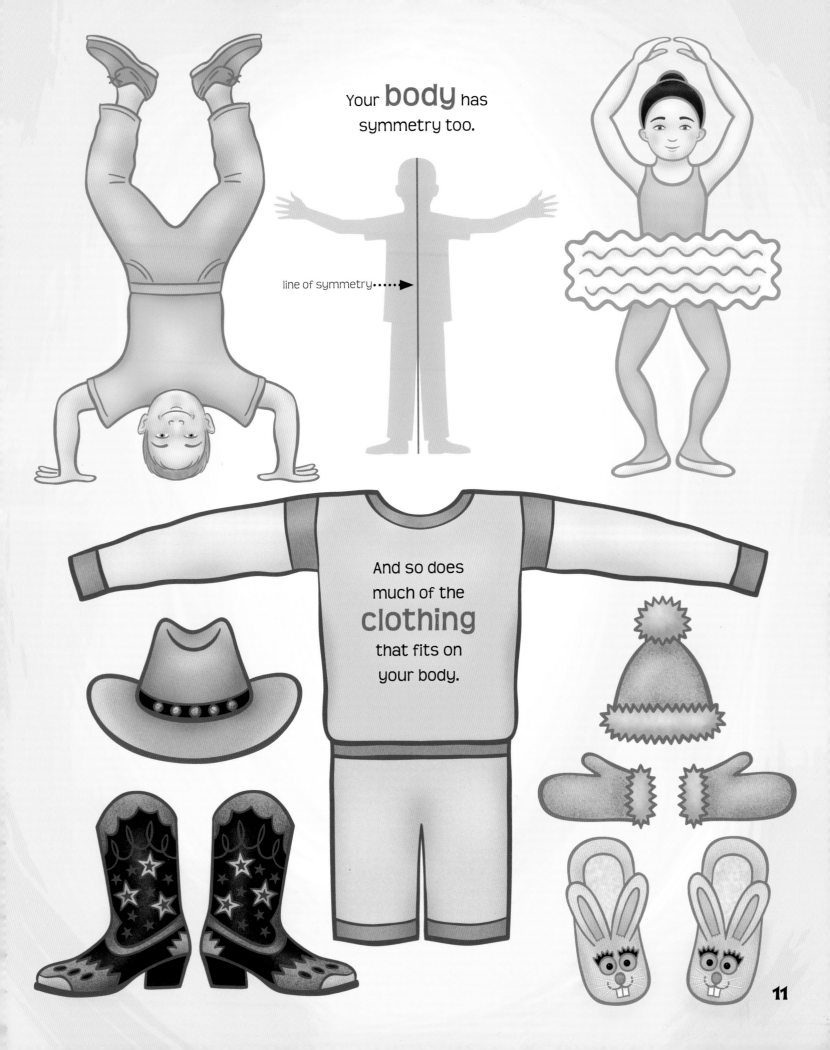

Your **body** has symmetry too.

line of symmetry ·····▶

And so does much of the **clothing** that fits on your body.

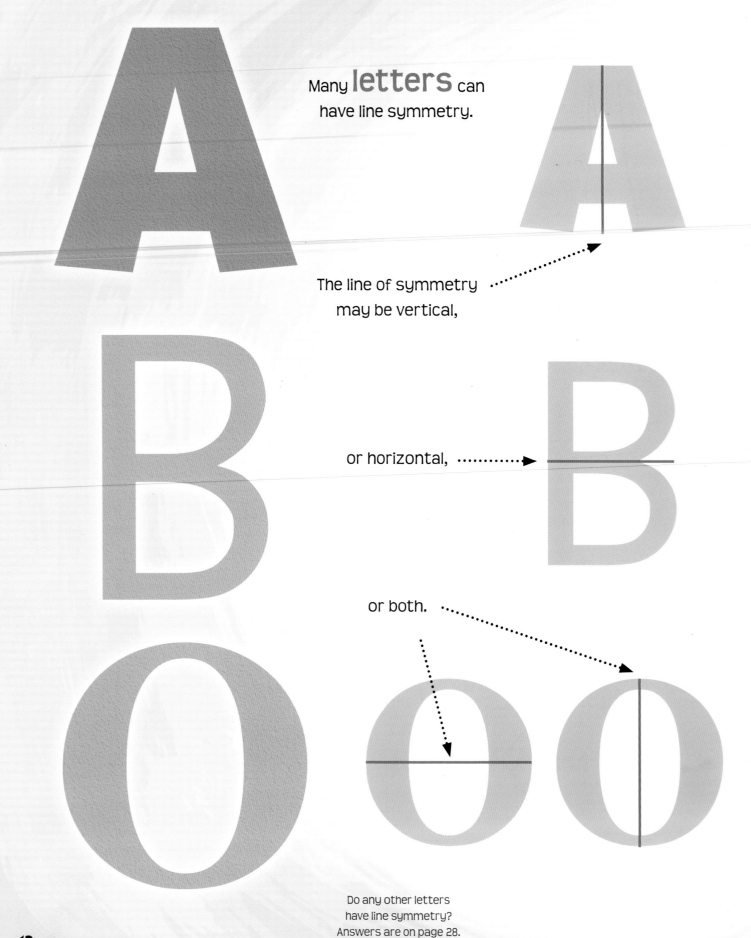

Many **letters** can have line symmetry.

The line of symmetry may be vertical,

or horizontal,

or both.

Do any other letters
have line symmetry?
Answers are on page 28.

Here are a few symmetrical **words.**

AHA

vertical line of symmetry

HID ~~HID~~

horizontal line of symmetry

MOM

CHICK

TOOT

COD

BOX

COOKIE

WOW

TUT

How many of these words
have a horizontal line
of symmetry?
See page 28.

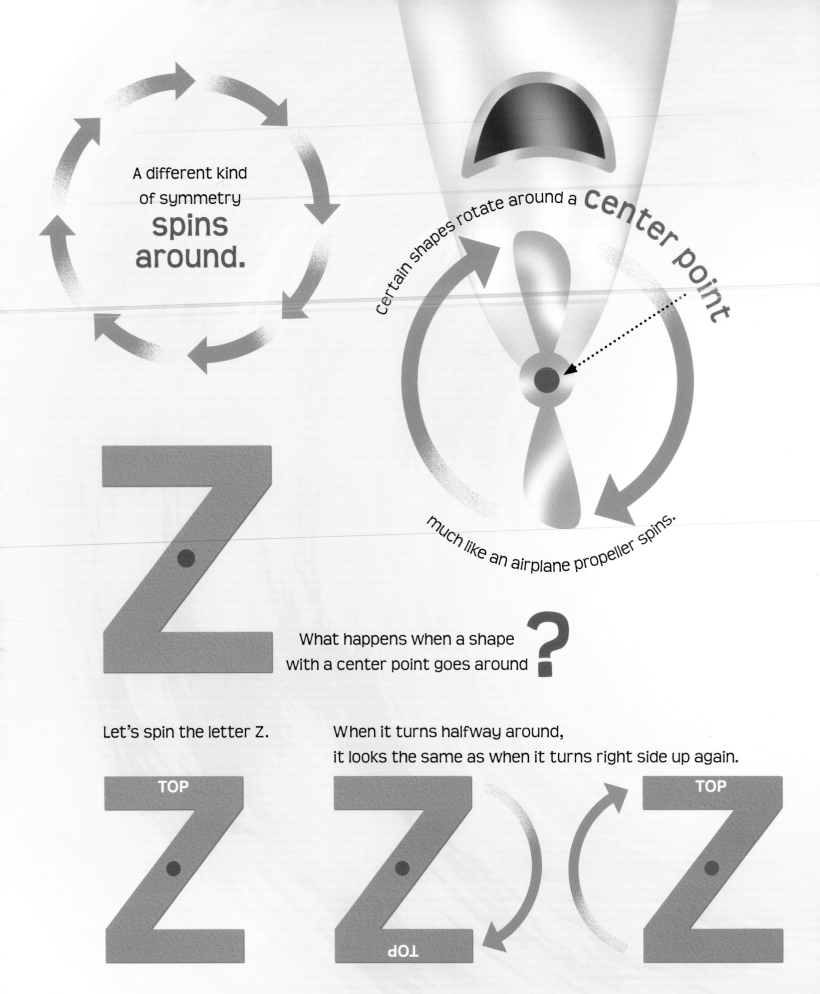

A different kind
of symmetry
**spins
around.**

Certain shapes rotate around a **center point**

much like an airplane propeller spins.

What happens when a shape
with a center point goes around **?**

Let's spin the letter Z.

When it turns halfway around,
it looks the same as when it turns right side up again.

TOP

TOP

TOP

How many letters have a center point? See page 29.

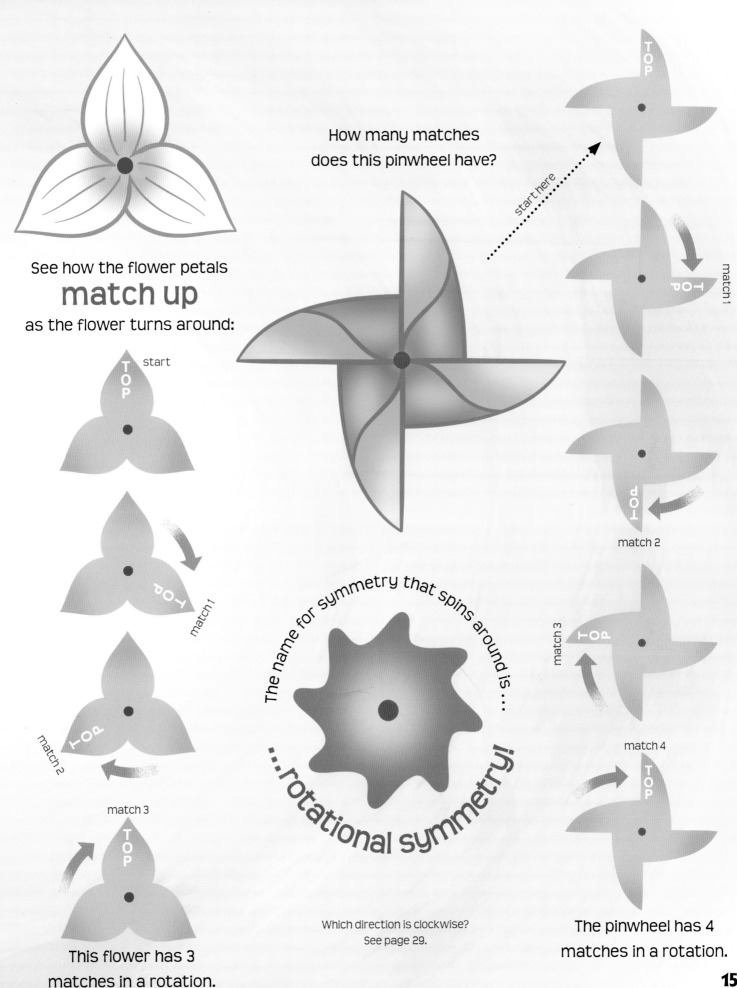

See how the flower petals
match up
as the flower turns around:

start

match 1

match 2

match 3

This flower has 3
matches in a rotation.

How many matches
does this pinwheel have?

start here

match 1

match 2

match 3

match 4

The pinwheel has 4
matches in a rotation.

The name for symmetry that spins around is ...
...rotational symmetry!

Which direction is clockwise?
See page 29.

stars

flowers

Rotational symmetry is found in nature and in things people make.

hubcaps

quilt blocks

Have you ever cut a paper shape
with rotational symmetry?

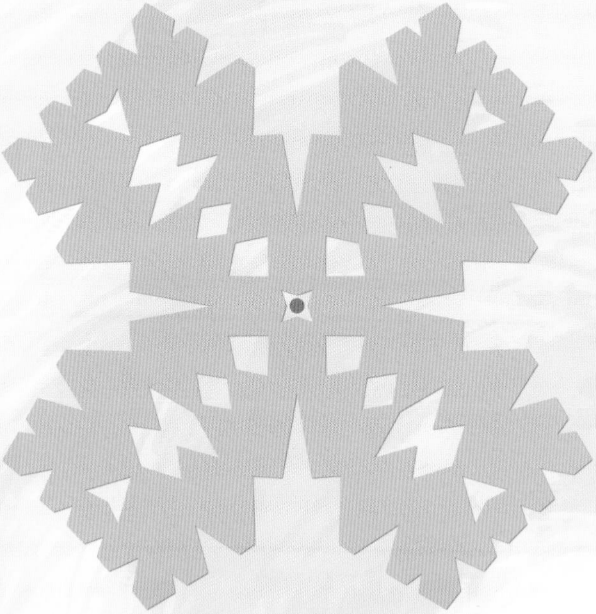

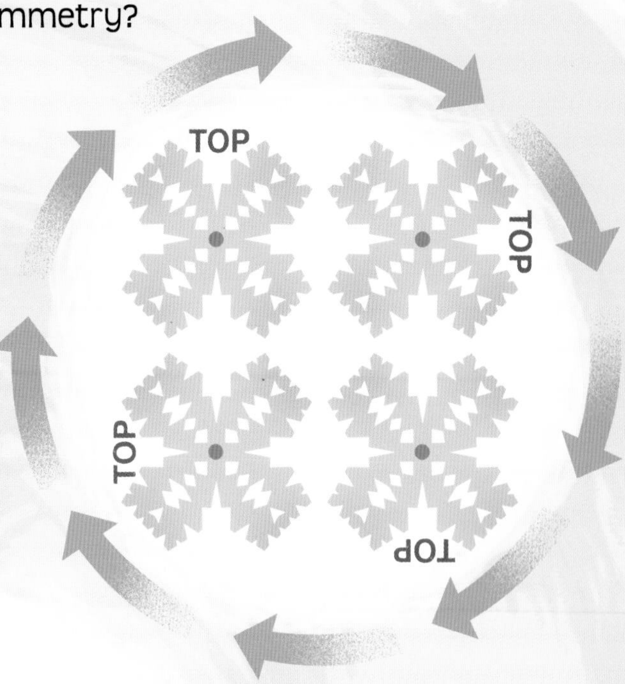

TOP

TOP

TOP

TOP

You can find
spectacular symmetry
when you look at a
snowflake

or inside a
kaleidoscope.

Do some of these shapes
have line symmetry too?
See page 29.

Animals in **motion** need symmetry to:

crawl,

swim,

hop,

walk,

run,

or fly!

Most animals move by using their legs, fins, or wings, which are mirror image pairs.

These animal bodies have line symmetry, but some life forms have rotational symmetry. See a few on page 29.

18

Many machines have symmetrical parts that rotate.

helicopter

gears

bicycle

wind turbine

waterwheel

Mexican paper-cut banner

medieval stained glass

Since ancient times, people have used symmetry in **art.**

Mimbres pottery

mask from Cameroon

Pennsylvania German fraktur painting

Haida totem pole

Chinese lattice

wood marquetry

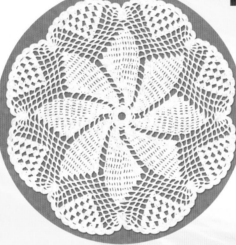

crocheted doily

How is this design made? See page 29.

Japanese temari ball

Turkish kilim rug

New Year's Eve

Valentine's Day

You may see symmetry
in many **holiday**
symbols and decorations.

St. Patrick's Day

Easter

Independence Day

Halloween

Hanukkah

Thanksgiving Day

Christmas

Which images have
rotational symmetry?
See page 29.

Many **buildings** have symmetry.

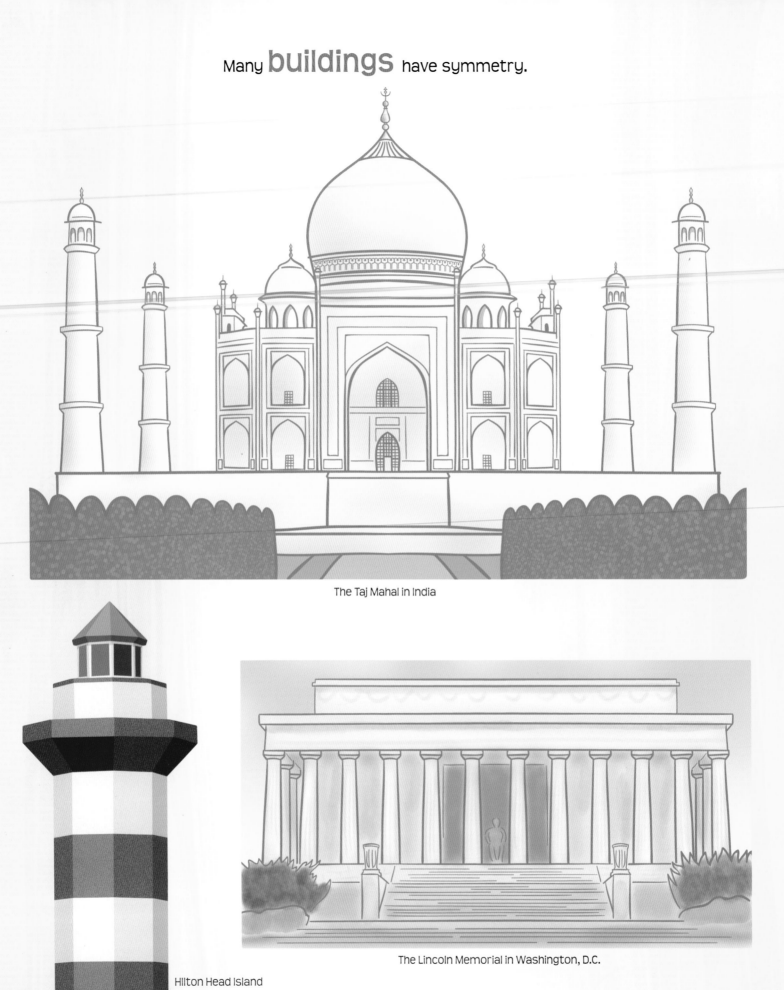

The Taj Mahal in India

Hilton Head Island
lighthouse

The Lincoln Memorial in Washington, D.C.

Most furniture does too.

Does anything on these two pages have rotational symmetry?
See page 29.

So now you'll spot the **symmetry:**

in the round,

up or down,

on your feet,

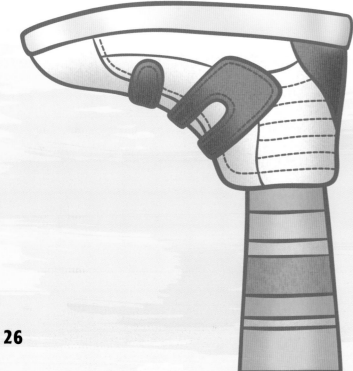

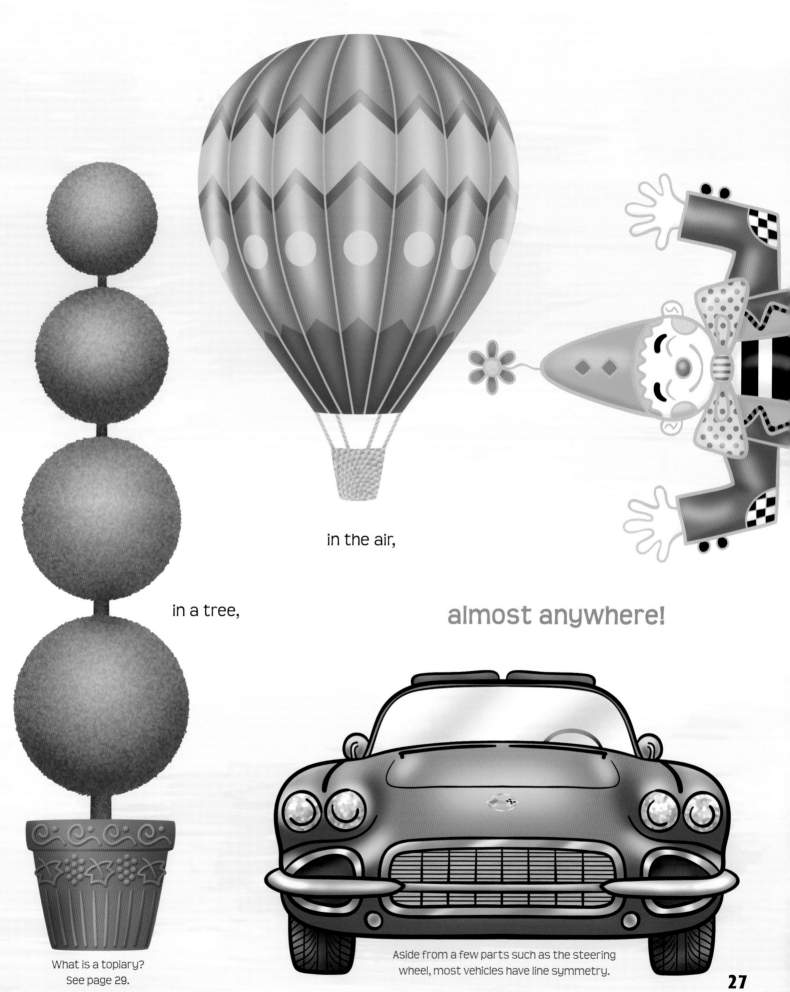

in the air,

in a tree,

almost anywhere!

What is a topiary?
See page 29.

Aside from a few parts such as the steering
wheel, most vehicles have line symmetry.

Notes

Page 7 Other terms for line symmetry are mirror symmetry, bilateral symmetry, and reflection symmetry.

Page 9 A few animals have bodies that are not symmetrical. The fiddler crab has one front claw that is much larger than its other one. More examples are the narwhal (a whale with a very long tusk on one side), the flounder (a fish with both eyes on the same side), the wonky-eyed squid (one of its eyes is much bigger), many types of shells (such as the conch), and hermit crabs (their bodies are twisted to allow them to fit into a shell).

Sponges are often irregular in shape and have no symmetry (so they are *asymmetrical*). Domestic animals such as cows, cats, and dogs often have very asymmetrical markings such as irregular spots. Wild animal markings such as tiger stripes aren't exactly alike on each side but are basically symmetrical.

Page 10 The structure of a human face has line symmetry—one eye, one eyebrow, and one ear are on either side of a line of symmetry that runs down the middle of the nose. The same is true of our bodies—each arm and leg has a mirror image arm and leg on the other side of the body.

Nobody's face or body is exactly symmetrical—if one ear is higher than the other, one cheek is wider than the other, and so on, these small variations add up to make each half a little different. The *insides* of animal and human bodies have asymmetrical parts—in humans, the heart and stomach are located on the left side, for example.

Page 12 Below are the capital letters that have line symmetry, either vertical, horizontal, or both:

fiddler crab

flounder

ABCDEHIKMOTUVWXY

The symmetry in letters can be lost due to the style of lettering used, as shown by this letter A (Times).

A

B

This Old English letter B has lost its symmetry too.

Page 13 The five words with a horizontal line of symmetry are:

HID CHICK COD BOX COOKIE

28

Page 14 The letters with rotational symmetry are:

Page 15 Clockwise means to spin to the right in the same direction the hands of a clock move. Counterclockwise means to spin to the left.

Pages 16-17 Some shapes have only rotational symmetry, such as the hubcaps, while some shapes have both line *and* rotational symmetry, such as the snowflake. See diagrams below:

This shape spins around a center point but has no line of symmetry (no mirror image halves).

This shape can spin around a center point AND it has 3 lines of symmetry.

1

3   2

Page 18 These microscopic diatoms, jellyfish, and starfish are examples of life forms with rotational symmetry.

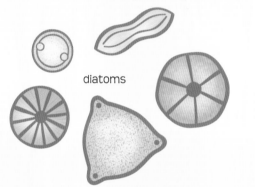

diatoms

jellyfish

starfish

Page 21 Native peoples of the Pacific Northwest carved totem poles, often with symmetrical designs. The fish near the top departs from the overall symmetry, as artists may choose to do at times.

A temari ball is made by wrapping different colors of thread around a sphere. Careful measuring creates the symmetrical patterns.

Pages 22-23 The colors of the eggs in the Easter basket are not symmetrical, though the positions of the eggs are.

The holiday images with rotational symmetry are the Independence Day stars, the wreath, the gift bow, and the star of David for Hanukkah.

Pages 24-25 The sofa pattern has rotational symmetry, as do the lamp, the rug, domes, towers, and columns as seen from above.

Page 27 A *topiary* is a tree or bush clipped into a decorative shape. Topiaries are often symmetrical.

As you look around your world, have fun seeing symmetry!

Symmetry Activities

Make a Symme-TREE!

Supplies: paper, pencil, and scissors

1 Fold a piece of paper in half the long way.

2 Draw half a tree along the fold line.

Here are some shapes to try:

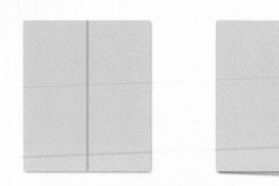

3 With your paper still folded, cut out the tree.

4 Open up and add some leaves, fruit, or flowers if you like.

Paint Blot Pattern

Supplies: a square piece of paper and several colors of creamy paint

1 Fold the paper in half vertically and then horizontally, pressing firmly to crease.

2 Place blobs of paint on the paper.

3 Fold the paper one way, pressing down to spread the paint. Open carefully and then fold the paper the other way.

4 Open the paper and allow the paint to dry.

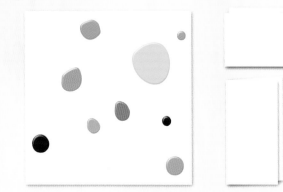 

For reproducible symmetry coloring pages and additional activities, please visit www.LoreenLeedy.com.

Why is symmetry an important MATH concept?

Mathematics is about more than numbers—it's also the study of **patterns, order,** and **comparisons.**

Math often involves finding patterns that **repeat.** Every type of symmetry must have a part that is repeated at least once.

Repeats are related to the math concept of **equality.** When something has symmetry, one part is equal to at least one other part. (It may be a mirror image, as in line symmetry.) Figuring out if something is equal often requires **measuring.**

Transformations are ways of moving shapes to make a repeated pattern. Transformations include **flips, turns,** and/or **slides.** A *flip* creates a mirror image as in line symmetry while a *turn* is the way rotational symmetry is formed.

Slides (or *glides*) are one or more moves along a straight line. They are not covered in this book but are often found in symmetrical patterns on wallpaper, gift wrap, and fabric. The flowers below are arranged in a sliding pattern.

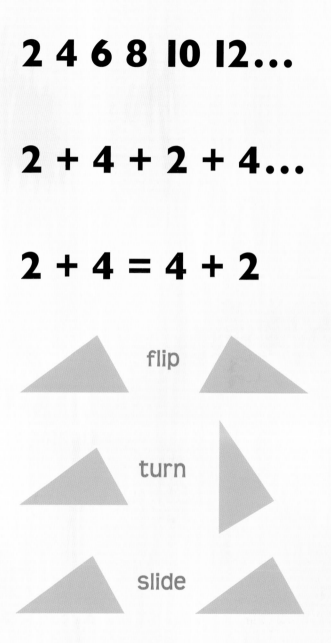

2 4 6 8 10 12...

2 + 4 + 2 + 4...

2 + 4 = 4 + 2

flip

turn

slide

Symmetry shows many math concepts in vivid, visual form.

The author wishes to thank Martha H. Hopkins, PhD and NBCT, of the College of Education at the University of Central Florida, for commenting on the text and sketches.

Symmetry Words

asymmetrical	(ay-suh-MEH-trih-kul) lacking symmetry
bilateral symmetry	same as **line symmetry**
clockwise	turning to the right (as a clock's hands turn)
counterclockwise	turning to the left
flip	to reverse a shape by turning it over (see **reflection**)
horizontal	going from side to side
line of symmetry	a straight line that divides a shape exactly in half
line symmetry	symmetry created when each half of a shape is a mirror image of the other
match	two shapes that are exactly the same
mirror symmetry	same as **line symmetry**
point	one spot
reflection	a mirror image (see **flip**)
reflection symmetry	same as **line symmetry**
rotate	to spin around a center point (same as **turn**)
rotational symmetry	symmetry formed by a shape that matches itself at least twice while turning
symmetrical	(suh-MEH-trih-kul) having symmetry
symmetry	(SIH-muh-tree) having equal parts in two or more directions
transformation	moving a shape into a different position
turn	to rotate around a center point (same as **rotate**)
vertical	going up and down

To Andy, my other half

This books meets the Common Core State Standards for fourth-grade mathematics in geometry: identify line-symmetric figures and draw lines of symmetry (4.G.3).

The publisher would like to thank Grace Wilkie for reviewing this book for accuracy.
Grace is the past president of the Association of Mathematics Teachers of New York State and New York State Mathematics Honor Society as well as an expert on Common Core Standards, National Council of Teachers of Mathematics Standards, and New York State Mathematics Standards.

Text and illustrations copyright © 2012 by Loreen Leedy
All rights reserved
HOLIDAY HOUSE is registered in the U.S. Patent and Trademark Office.
Printed and Bound in November 2011 at Kwong Fat Offset Printing Co., Ltd.,
Dongguan City, China.
The art for this book was created in Adobe Illustrator and Photoshop.
The text typeface is Teen.
www.holidayhouse.com
First Edition
1 3 5 7 9 10 8 6 4 2

Library of Congress Cataloging-in-Publication Data
Leedy, Loreen.
Seeing Symmetry / by Loreen Leedy. — 1st ed.
p. cm.
ISBN 978-0-8234-2360-6 (hardcover)
1. Symmetry—Juvenile literature.
2. Ratio and proportion—Juvenile literature.
I. Title.
Q172.5.S95L44 2012
516'.1—dc23
2011024038

J
516.1
LEE